W9-AXC-879

Bv

Water Pollution

Water
Pollution

Andrew Donnelly

T H E   C H I L D ' S   W O R L D®, INC.

8463622

Copyright © 1999 by The Child's World®, Inc.
All rights reserved. No part of this book may be
reproduced or utilized in any form or by any means
without written permission from the publisher.
Printed in the United States of America.

Library of Congress Cataloging-in-Publication Data
Donnelly, Andrew.
Water pollution / by Andrew Donnelly.
p.   cm.
Includes index.
Summary: Questions and answers introduce the basics
of water pollution, its causes, effects, and prevention.
ISBN 1-56766-510-1 (library reinforced : alk. paper)
1. Water pollution—Juvenile literature.
2. Water quality management—Juvenile literature.
[1. Water pollution—Miscellanea. 2. Pollution—Miscellanea
3. Questions and answers.]   I. Title.
TD422.D66   1998
363.739'4—dc21   97-31352
CIP
AC

Photo Credits

© 1995 Barbara Gerlach/Dembinsky Photo Assoc. Inc: 30
© Bill Pogue/Tony Stone Images: 23
© David Woodfall/Tony Stone Worldwide: 24
© H. Richard Johnston/Tony Stone Worldwide: 10
© Joseph Sterling/Tony Stone Worldwide: 26
© 1997 John Mielcarek/Dembinsky Photo Assoc. Inc: 19
© 1992 John Mielcarek/Dembinsky Photo Assoc. Inc: 20
© 1993 John Mielcarek/Dembinsky Photo Assoc. Inc: 9
© 1994 John S. Botkin/Dembinsky Photo Assoc. Inc: 15
© 1997 Marilyn Kazmers/Dembinsky Photo Assoc. Inc: 2
© NASA: 6
© 1993 Ted Nelson/Dembinsky Photo Assoc. Inc: cover
© Randy Wells/Tony Stone Images: 16
© 1992 Stan Osolinski/Dembinsky Photo Assoc. Inc: 29
© Tony Stone Images: 13

On the cover...

Front cover: Trash has made this Michigan pond very ugly.
Page 2: Litter like this makes water unsafe.

Table of Contents

What Is Water Pollution?

If you could travel through outer space in a spaceship, you would find other wonderful worlds circling our Sun. Some are huge, colorful balls of gas. Others are small, hot, and rocky. The most interesting world, though, is our own blue and green planet, Earth. It has something none of the other planets have. What could that be? It's flowing water!

From high above, Earth's water looks clean and beautiful. But if you look at it closely, you can see that much of it is not clean. In fact, it is so dirty that many plants and animals cannot live in it! Garbage and other things that make water harmful to life are called **water pollution**.

This pipe is dumping polluted water into a small pond. ⇒

Are There Different Types of Water?

Earth has two types of water. *Saltwater,* which has a lot of salt in it, is found in the oceans and seas. Almost all of Earth's water is saltwater.

Freshwater has very little salt in it. It is found in lakes, ponds, rivers, and streams. *Groundwater* is freshwater that lies deep underground. Most people drink groundwater. They find it by digging wells.

⇐ Freshwater splashes down this waterfall.

Why Is Water Important?

Every living thing on Earth needs water. In fact, plants and animals are made mostly of water! Without water, every living thing would die. Many plants and animals make their homes in water. Even plants and animals that live on land need water to drink. Water is very important.

Like all other animals, these zebras need water to live. ⇒

Water also causes much of our weather. When the water in a lake or ocean heats up, it **evaporates**, or rises into the air. Slowly, the evaporated water forms clouds that circle the Earth. Sometimes the water in a cloud becomes too heavy. When this happens, the water falls out of the cloud as rain or snow.

These clouds are full of water. ⇒

We use water in many ways. We use it for cleaning and cooking. We use it to wash our clothes and our bodies. We even use it to flush our toilets. But the most important way we use water is by drinking it. Without water, we could stay alive only for a few days.

We need water outside of our homes, too. Farmers and gardeners need water for their crops. Factories use water to cool machines and mix chemicals. Water is even used to make electricity. We build dams that trap the power of running water and turn it into electricity. This kind of power is called **hydroelectric power**.

⇐ Dams like this one are used to make electricity.

What Causes Water Pollution?

People often dump garbage into rivers, lakes, and the ocean. They think the garbage will float away and disappear. Instead, it stays in the water. If there is too much garbage in the water, it can kill the fish and plants that live there. It also can harm other animals that need the water to drink.

Besides garbage, heat can also cause water pollution. When factories dump hot water into lakes and streams, the rest of the water heats up. Plants and animals cannot live in water that gets too warm.

Fish and other animals cannot live in this polluted pond. ⇒

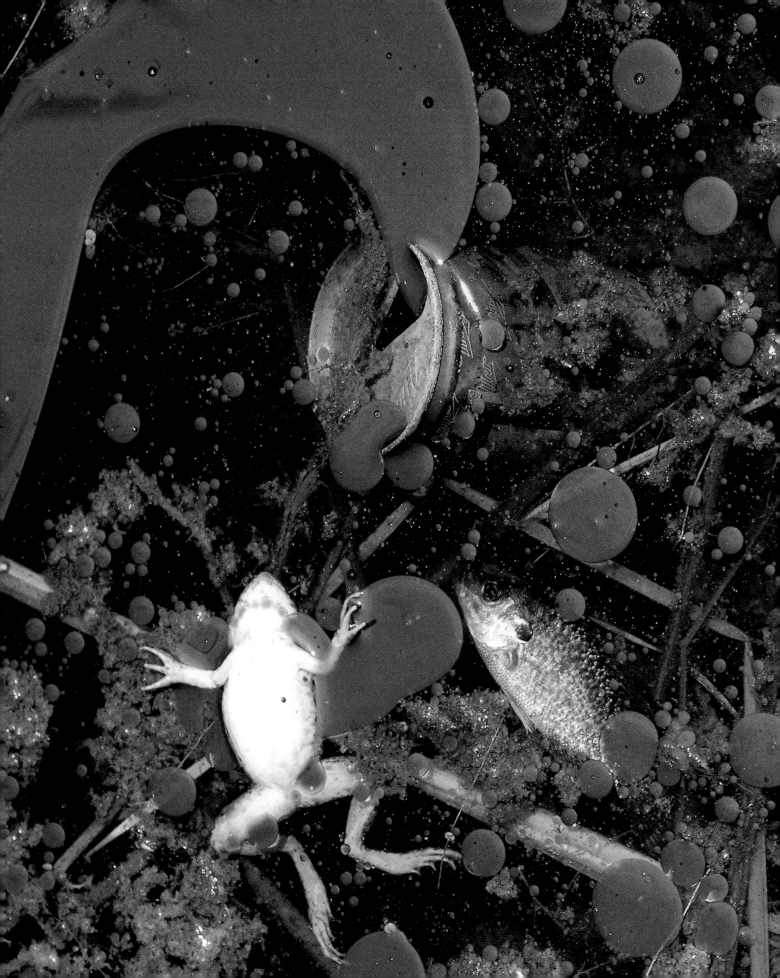

The most serious water pollution comes from **chemicals**. We use thousands of kinds of chemicals. They make up fertilizers, cleaners, insect poisons, and countless products we use every day. Even your shampoo is made of chemicals! When chemicals are dumped into the water, some can harm plants and animals. Even when they are dumped on land, they can soak into the ground and pollute the groundwater.

Does Water Pollution Cause Damage?

Tires, plastic bags, cans, fishing line, and old clothes are just some of the kinds of garbage found in our lakes and streams. Every year, thousands of birds and other animals die when they eat trash or get trapped in it.

This shoreline in Texas is covered with trash. ⇒

Chemicals in the water can cause even worse damage. Once chemicals get into the water, it is very hard to get them out. In rivers and lakes, chemical pollution sometimes causes tiny living things called **bacteria** to grow. Some bacteria can make other things sick or even kill them.

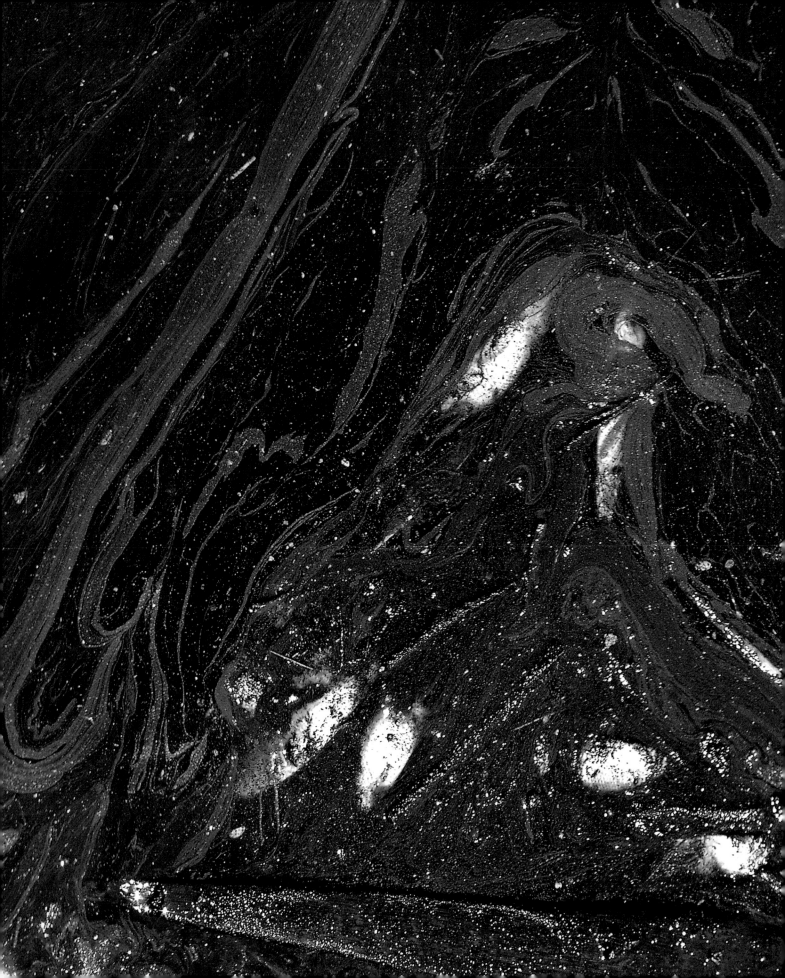

One of the most harmful chemicals is oil. When oil leaks into the water, it destroys many things. It kills fish and animals that live in the water. It harms other animals that eat the ocean's fish and plants. It even destroys plants, trees, and animals that live near the shore! That is why ships carrying oil must try to avoid causing oil spills.

Is Water Pollution Dangerous?

Water pollution can be very dangerous. It can affect all living things, from plants to people, and make them sick. Everything on Earth needs clean water to stay healthy.

Animals like this moose need clean water every day. ⇒

Can We Stop Water Pollution?

Today, many countries have laws that protect Earth's water. These laws help, but there is still much more we can do. It is up to all of us to protect our water. We can help by picking up trash and putting it where it belongs. We must also be careful with chemicals. If we keep our water clean, Earth will still look as beautiful close up as it does from outer space!

Glossary

bacteria (bak–TEER–ee–uh)
Bacteria are very tiny living things. Some bacteria can make people, plants, and animals sick.

chemicals (KEH–mih–kulz)
Chemicals are substances that make up products we use every day, including cleaners, paints, and fertilizers. Sometimes chemicals get into the water and cause pollution.

evaporate (ee–VAH–puh–rayt)
When water evaporates, it rises into the air as a gas. Evaporated water often forms clouds.

hydroelectric power (HY–droh ee–LEK–trik POW-er)
Hydroelectric power uses running water to create electricity.

water pollution (WAH–ter puh–LOO–shun)
Water pollution happens when garbage and other things make water harmful to life. Water pollution is a serious problem all over the world.

Index